SURRENDERING THE HEART OF A FATHER

*A Man's Discussion Guide to
Abortion Recovery*

Mike and Pat Layton

CONTENTS

DEDICATION

This book is dedicated to men who have been involved, directly or indirectly, in the loss of an innocent son or daughter, due to an abortion decision.

I have learned since my own abortion with my wife Pat, Author of Surrendering the Secret, just how many lives abortion effects. Sisters, brothers, grandparents, aunts and uncles...the ripple effect goes on and on. To help us understand this massive loss consider this truth—World War I, World War II, the Korean War and the Viet Nam War combined, yielded a total of 121.2 Million casualties. The World Health Organization estimates there are 56 MILLION abortions performed around the world every single year. It is difficult to imagine that during just the first 3 years of legalized abortion, we have destroyed more lives than all of these wars combined. As a Marine Veteran, these startling facts hit hard.

It is not difficult to encounter the passionate political and social debate that surrounds the topic of abortion. This study will enter no such debate instead stands upon a pro-life; pro-love, faith based position of healing the heartbreak and shame that often surrounds an abortion experience.

It is estimated that a woman speaks 20,000 words per day compared to a man's average of 7,000. We have written this discussion booklet to reach men.

God speed and my prayers as you search for God's complete healing and your abundant and free life.

Mike Layton
stsfathersheart@gmail.com
John 10:10

IF YOU ARE THE FATHER OF AN ABORTED CHILD, WHAT TO DO RIGHT NOW!

1. Confess your loss or sin to God and ask Him to move you out of darkness, lead your path to healing and into His Kingdom work. (Revelation 12;11)

2. Healing is always best in community. Seek out a mature Christian friend, counselor or pastor to join you on this journey. (James 5:16)

3. Contact us at stsfathersheart@gmail.com   We have several resources available for men, women and couples:

Surrendering the Secret (lifeway.com/Bible Study)
A Surrendered Life (amazon.com) This is the chapter version of Surrendering the Secret.
Support videos made with women sharing their stories through each step of this healing process are available from lifeway.com. Men's videos are coming soon!

This short study guide can be used alone or with one of the above resources.

Contact us at www.surrenderingthesecret.com or stsinternational15@gmail.com for questions or support.

We have men on our team to answer your questions.

"Take no part in unfruitful works of darkness, but instead expose them."
Ephesians 5:11

"When I kept silent about my sin, my body wasted away through my groaning all day long."
Psalm 32:3

If we say that we have no sin, we are deceiving ourselves and the truth is not in us. If we confess our sins, He is faithful and righteous to forgive us our sins and to cleanse us from all unrighteousness.
1 John 1:8-9

Therefore, confess your sins to one another, and pray for one another so that you may be healed.
James 5:16

This booklet can be used alone, with a friend or pastor or with a spouse or significant other. We strongly recommend sharing this journey with at least one other spiritual mentor or partner. Although a small group setting is ideal it is not always easy for men to join other men, they don't know to pursue post abortion recovery in the same way women do. First of all, men respond to the emotions of an abortion differently and often lump the loss and shame they might feel into other perceived "failures" of the past. It's difficult at first to open up about their past behaviors, share their feelings and thoughts or take part in a "group" chat setting. It takes a great deal of courage and humility for a man to make himself vulnerable emotionally and spiritually. However, when they do, in a short period of time, trust and bonding can build, and honest dialogue of sharing feelings and emotions are expressed. Some men share more openly, easily and at times passionately while others suppress their feelings.

After a few weeks of gathering, deep personal feelings begin to be shared. Hardened hearts and offenses begin softening and evidence of the healing process can occur.

For some men the healing is deeper and more profound than for other men. God is at work transforming each of their hearts filling these men with hope, wisdom, and discernment and bringing to the surface a repentant spirit and confession of sin. It is a life changing experience to watch 1 John 1:9 come to life on the faces of these men.

"When you confess your sin, God is faithful and just to forgive your sin and cleanse you of all unrighteousness."

As trust, confidence and insight build, men start questioning and maybe even confronting one another. In most cases this is done lovingly and respectfully and received very well. As they begin to operate as a team, building unity and praying for each other, the healing process takes place.

Conversation and interaction increase, stuffed memories and emotions are released, and detailed personal experiences and testimonies are shared.

This booklet can serve as a one on one or group discussion guide that will share an example of answered questions and result in a personal response.

ABORTION HURTS MEN TOO

As more women respond to the healing journey of a past abortion, God is clearly stirring the hearts of men across the nation as well. Through our leadership team at *Surrendering the Secret*, calls and emails come in on a regular basis seeking someone to talk to who understands the loss of fatherhood caused by abortion. Abortion is the antithesis to all God created, called, equipped, and empowered men to do and experience in life!

Men really want to provide for and protect others, especially their women and children. Most men tend to fix things, stuff things, and control things yet they also want to succeed and accomplish things.

How do men deal and cope with a past abortion?

The answer is in multiple ways! Men experience many emotions and start acting out in multiple ways to deal with the pain, guilt, and grief and inability to protect their child including:

Stuffing feelings: No feeling

Alcohol abuse

Anxiety

Withdrawing

Struggle with close relationships

Drug use

Depression

Cynicism and/or anger issues

Multiple unhealthy relationships

No motivation to excel

Feeling like failure

Low self-worth

Disdain for women

Men who originally agreed with or even pressed for abortion often bury their feelings and behavior by justifying their decision. Not so different from women, here are a few common rationalizations:

- It was legal and best for everyone
- We can't afford a child right now
- Everybody has abortions, it's not a big deal
- The timing wasn't right to get married
- We hardly knew each other

Men don't like to fail or feel helpless, hopeless, trapped, out of control or let others down especially family, friends and an unborn child! When a man experiences an abortion that he did not want to happen, everything inside him cries out "failure!" In the case of a man who wasn't able to save and protect his child, anger and resentment begin to build.

Anger often results in:

- Hurt
- Injustice
- Fear
- Offense
- Shame
- Frustration.

Whether alone or in a group, when men take the time to take this healing journey they are filled with scripture, self-revealing insights and truth that sets them free from guilt and shame. Greater and deeper signs of healing and forgiveness are revealed to the point that the men become more transparent, about other things in life and experience God's love and grace. Transformation takes place in these men through the power of the Holy Spirit helping them to fulfill God's calling and destiny in their lives. By the end of this healing process you will feel forgiven and empowered experiencing the Joy of the Lord!

It is a simple fact that conception of a child requires the equal biological participation of a female and a male counterpart—a mother and a father. The baby is obviously the first victim in abortion. Moreover, the pro-life community has leaned toward spotlighting the mother as a victim while often down-playing or even ignoring the fact that the baby's father is also a victim of the lies of a culture that advocates abortion. The Roe v Wade Supreme Court decision of 1973 violently slung the door open for widespread legalized abortion in the U.S. The court focused on the woman's right to privacy while the personhood of the child in the womb was disregarded. So were the rights of the father.

In the immediate years following this decision, many states adopted laws protecting the rights of men by requiring the husband's consent before his wife could follow through with an abortion. Soon after the Supreme Court evaluated those state laws, and deemed them inconsistent with the basis and decision of the Roe v Wade case, and therefore, unconstitutional.

Here we are decades later, millions and millions of men have been affected by abortion. Many have knowingly participated in abortions through a wide range of approaches, from passivity to coercion. Many others were uninformed, deceived or may have fought unsuccessfully for the lives of their unborn children.

Extensive research on the subject of men who have been harmed by abortion. In her book, *Men and Abortion: A Path to Healing*, by Dr Catherine Coyle, a man called Dan recounts the inner turmoil he experienced in accompanying his future wife during an abortion. Helplessness and confusion were two common themes expressed by the men interviewed in Coyle's research.

"My paternal instincts began kicking in, but I didn't show it. In my heart, I wanted to somehow stop the procedure and save the baby. I felt so helpless. I rubbed and rubbed her stomach thinking I could soothe the baby, or at least let it know it was loved, if just for a short time. I wanted to hold it. I wanted to hug it. I wanted it to live, like the baby chicks and rabbits I had nursed back to life as a child. I wanted to die in its place. Sadness overcame every muscle in my body. It was just so sad!"

– Dan, post-abortion father

The state laws related to abortion disregard the father, thereby communicating that the father has no final influence or authority. They are, therefore, denied the paternal instinct that motivates them to care for their families. One post-abortion father who now counsels post-abortion men wrote, "As I reflect on God's purpose and role for men, I see that because of my choice of participating in this offensive sin of killing my unborn child, I quit life. I taught myself to shortcut life in all decisions in the future (husband decisions, father decisions, job decisions, etc.)."

What makes things worse is that men are more likely than women to go forward in denial about negative emotions profoundly affecting their lives. Vincent Rue, Ph.D., a forerunner in researching the effects of abortion on men, wrote, "Men do grieve following abortion, but they are more likely to deny their grief or internalize their feelings of loss rather than openly express them . . . When men do express their grief, they try to do so in culturally prescribed 'masculine 'ways, i.e. anger, aggressiveness, control." Men who have partnered in an abortion often experience tendencies toward angry and violent behavior as well as an overall sense of lost manhood. Common consequences include broken relationships; sexual dysfunction; substance abuse; self-hatred; ever-increasing feelings of grief, guilt, and depression; as well as dangerous and even suicidal behavior.

King David describes the body's reaction to secret sin:

When I kept silent about my sin, my body wasted away through my groaning all day long. Psalm 32:3

John's first epistle stressed the importance of confession:

If we say that we have no sin, we are deceiving ourselves and the truth is not in us. If we confess our sins, He is faithful and righteous to forgive us our sins and to cleanse us from all unrighteousness. 1 John 1:8-9

James 5:16 takes confession even farther:

Therefore, confess your sins to one another, and pray for one another so that you may be healed.

One has to wonder what would happen if there was widespread confession of this sin that has ravaged the nation. What would happen if mighty warriors, expressing strength through weakness, stepped into the front lines creating a massive wave of confession and repentance? How would marriages be affected in the here and now? How would this culture be affected as a whole? Would the hearts of the fathers be turned back to the children?

What if, rather than hiding the truth of past and present sexual impurity, confessions and repentance became an igniting fire in our churches? What about those men living in the fortress of a heart hardened by the deceitfulness of sin, self-justification and resentment? The shame, guilt and blame can be so deep-rooted these wounded warriors more often than not need fellow soldiers and armor bearers to fight alongside them.

Perhaps the real question is, "What would happen if men fought back?" Not with weapons of the flesh. But as Paul wrote in 2 Corinthians 10:3-4, "*For though we walk in the flesh, we do not war according to the flesh, for the weapons of our warfare are not of the flesh, but divinely powerful for the destruction of fortresses.*"

When a man struggles with sin, he is likely to keep his secret. However, biblical wisdom tells him not to give in to fear, pride and shame. Forgiveness and healing is achievable. Be a warrior; go after your victory!

The following is a variety of responses gathered from various sources from men who were interviewed or ask about their personal experience in an abortion decision. This collection is not intended to serve as an all-inclusive list; rather, an overview of possible scenarios and reactions that men might have to an abortion experience.

1. The father who was adamantly opposed to the procedure.

This man may have an immediate and overwhelming response. It is hard for him to separate the feelings he is experiencing, but they include grief, guilt, rage/anger, and a sense of male impotence, ie, he couldn't protect his partner or his child. He may be inclined to make repeated contact with his partner in an effort to understand how the decision was made.

2. The father who was opposed but did not go to extremes to prevent it.

This man may also have an immediate reaction including sadness, grief and a sense of not being able to protect. He may experience anger, but not full blown rage, as well as the other emotions listed above. He is not as prone to a violent reaction to his grief.

3. The father who first supported the abortion decision and then changed his mind.

This man holds himself responsible in a special way because he agreed and then changed his mind. So, the abortion progressed anyway. This seems to happen within marriages more frequently. This can become an issue within the relationship that interferes with basic trust and can interfere with intimate couple relations.

4. The father who appeared to be neutral on the issue.

This man supported the choice of the mother. Some men are actually opposed but society has urged him to be supportive of her decision. Other men find the abortion decision to serve them well at a particular point in their lives.

The man who is unable to articulate how he really feels may react like the first two groups of men. The man who is truly in agreement or neutral in the abortion decision may not feel anything until years later.

5. The father who simply abandoned the woman in the face of pregnancy.

The man who abandoned may not be troubled by the event but may later find himself bothered by his behavior. This man may have several abortion experiences.

6. The father who forced the abortion decision or threatened to withdraw support if abortion was not chosen.

The man who forces the abortion decision may have many abortion losses in a lifetime. Often, the relationship that resulted in the abortion may no longer be active. The relationship may break apart because the woman and the man react differently. The woman who is forced into an abortion decision may have an immediate adverse reaction that the man may not be able to understand. He may tell her to "get over it" if she tries to speak of her confusion or discomfort. This undercuts the relationship. Her discomfort might also bother him and so the relationship might dissolve.

7. The father who was not told about the abortion until after it occurred.

This man may react with confusion, in that his partner did not discuss this matter with him but made a unilateral decision. It is possible that he might not find out until years later when a conversation with an acquaintance may bring the unfolding of the story. He experiences many conflicting emotions, wrestling with the strength of their relationship and the lack of trust. There is often much ambivalence and confusion experienced in these settings.

8. The father who is not certain an abortion has occurred, but upon hearing the description of post-abortion aftermath in women, recognize the symptoms in a former partner.

This man may wonder if there was a pregnancy that he was responsible for. He is unable to confirm that a pregnancy occurred. This can sometimes lead to many unanswered questions.

9. The man who married a woman who had an abortion experience with someone else.

This man may be engulfed in the vortex of the woman's reaction to her previous abortion(s). He may or may not have been told about the experience of abortion. He may be confused by what is happening with his partner and may be very concerned about her.

10. The man other than a sexual partner.

This man may have been aware of or actively participated in the decision to abort through a relationship with the mother or father who had the abortion. He may be a friend or a relative such as a brother or father. Many emotions are experienced by these men.

SURRENDERING THE HEART OF A FATHER

A MAN'S PERSPECTIVE

In an effort to adapt the group study platform used in Surrendering the Secret to provide a healing resource for men, we asked several men who had shared their past abortions with us, to complete these questions as they correlate with each of the Eight Steps to healing found in *Surrendering the Secret* and the companion book *A Surrendered Life.*.

All of our materials are interchangeable and support one another. Some material is duplicated one resource to another.

The following 8 steps of healing will be started with a discussion provoking question and one man's response.

They will serve as a guide for you to walk through and consider your own responses to each step.

VIDEO OPTION: *Surrendering the Secret* is a video driven bible study written for women. To take this journey on a deeper level you can download the available videos that go with each step in the woman's version of this same journey found in *Surrendering the Secret.* Watching and considering the responses to each of these steps by women will surely prompt a deeper response to each step.

Find videos at lifeway.com/surrenderingthesecret or Contact us at www.surrenderingthesecret.com or stsfathersheart@gmail.com for questions or support.

EIGHT STEPS TO HEALING FROM A PAST ABORTION

STEP ONE: Going Back to Get Ahead

Question #1
As a man, how do you handle memories of your past, especially things you are ashamed of or don't like to talk about?

Answer: Before I was healed of my abortion, I would never deal with the issue. If I were ever in a conversation where abortion even came up. For at least 9 of the 15 years I kept my abortion a secret and didn't talk about it at all, not to my wife, not to anyone. Then I had a rebirth in my relationship with Christ! Because of the revival in my life, I now had an attitude about abortion. Even though my wife and I were not completely healed and were still keeping our own secret, I remember feeling disgusted with the whole abortion scene! The truth is, I was angry with myself! For more than 6 years we had kept our secret and now that my Spirit was awakened, I was angry. I was angry at me. I was angry at her. I was angry at the whole world.

When my wife received healing on a ministry retreat weekend, our lives changed FOREVER! She came home and told me she was healed and had to tell everyone what the Lord had done for her and it meant telling the secret! At that point I was a little taken aback but I could not deny that I had a whole wife. She came home from that weekend better in every way. She was healed, at peace, and armed with purpose. With a passion for my wife like never before, I knew that what I had stolen from her those 15 years before had been restored and made better than new. I wanted that for myself as well.

Question #2
Read the story of Abraham/Sarah and Hagar in Gen 16:7-15 and share some thoughts of how Abraham handled this situation and how he might have felt about Hagar's suffering.

Answer: I'm not sure if Abraham was taking responsibility or not? Kind of looks like not, he threw the burden of decision right back to Sarah telling her to "do with her what you will". Like a lot of men, I surrendered my decision to someone else. I placed the burden on my wife. I let someone else dictate my life and the someone was not God. It was me. I was more worried about what people would think and say and about pleasing them than I was about pleasing the God who had blessed me with a new life. Like Abraham I took matters into my own hands, or rather DIDN'T take the responsibility for my actions I needed to take and made a mess of things.

Question #3
To this point in life, how have you dealt with the story of your aborted child or children, the woman involved, and your part in the choice? Is your story public? Who Knows? How have you shared your story?

Answer: At this point in my life my wife and I have embraced our abortion story together! We share the whole truth of our abortion so that others might make a better choice or be healed from a bad one. We also feel God wants us to share that abortion is not the unforgivable sin. God does not hate us, He loves us. He's not mad at us, He wants us to share the truth about abortion on His behalf. We tell others, old and young, that an unplanned pregnancy is not a death sentence. My wife and I have now been married for over 23 years and we thank God that through Him, we have beat the odds! She has forgiven me for my part in the abortion. Through working together and following the path of Surrendering the Secret, the purity and trust that I stole from her has been restored. Our story is very public. We are the founders and she is the director of "Lifetime Pregnancy Help Centre" in Springfield, Illinois. Our lives are dedicated to saving women, babies and men from the heartbreak of abortion. We started by telling our 5 children, our parents and our families. I was a Senior Associate Pastor at a local church when my wife received her healing. We asked the Senior Pastor if we could share our testimony with our entire congregation. Afterwards, men and women filled the alter to ask questions and receive prayer for their own past abortions. That was the beginning of a new ministry God had for us. Now, we share our story every day and thank God for every opportunity.

NOW IT's YOUR TURN!
Note Your Responses to these Questions:

Question #1 As a man, how do you handle memories of your past, especially things you are ashamed of or don't like to talk about?

_____

_____

_____

_____

_____

_____

_____

Question #2 Read the story of Abraham/Sarah and Hagar in Gen 16:7-15 and share some thoughts of how Abraham handled this situation and how he might have felt about Hagar's suffering.

_____

_____

_____

_____

_____

_____

_____

_____

Question #3 To this point in life, how have you dealt with the story of your aborted child or children, the woman involved, and your part in the choice? Is your story public?

_____

_____

Who Knows?

_____

_____

_____

_____

_____

How have you shared your story?

_____

_____

_____

_____

_____

_____

_____

_____

_____

_____

_____

_____

_____

_____

_____

_____

_____

_____

_____

_____

_____

_____

_____

_____

_____

_____

_____

_____

_____

_____

_____

_____

_____

_____

_____

STEP TWO---Share Your Story

Question #1: What were your life circumstances and relationships like at the time of your abortion?

Answer: I was 20 years old and living with my family out of state. My fiance' came to spend the summer and live with me before she went off to a enjoy a full college basketball scholarship. We were both working and living a nice life with no cares to speak of. Everything was just as we had planned. Until we discovered she was pregnant.

Question #2: Was there anyone in your life you felt you could completely trust?

Answer: As I look back on it now the only two people we told about the pregnancy were people I believed at the time we could trust. It turned out that the advice we received was not good. The influence to get an abortion was the order of the day.

Question #3: When or how did the idea of abortion come to mind? What other options did you consider?

Answer: Our first thoughts about abortion came through the advice of our friends. It all sounded logical and legitimate at the time. "This baby doesn't fit in the plan for your life right now!" "You can't have a baby you will lose your fifty thousand dollar, full ride scholarship!" "It's just not time right now you have your whole life ahead of you!". Unfortunately, we did not consider any other options we just did our best to hide the pregnancy and get the abortion behind us. Our plan was to get it over with as soon as possible and move on with the plan we had for our life.

Question #4: Describe your abortion experience.

Answer: From what I can remember It was a long quiet ride as I tried to comfort my fiancé and just be there for support. Somehow, even then, I knew deep down that I had broken her trust and wondered if things would or could ever be the same. I was just hoping that we could just move on with our lives and leave it all behind. My plan was never to think or deal with it again. I just wanted to do whatever I could to fix it. It didn't turn out that way, strangely enough I just took all the anger and disappointment from my fiancé and carried it every day with a smile on my face. Deep in my heart I was ashamed, and I knew I had lost her trust.

Question #5: Share thoughts and feelings you recall before, during and after the abortion.

Answer: The first thing I remember was disbelief. That test had to be wrong. We had barely been together. During the process of finding out the test was true I just kept thinking "how could I fix this?". We can have an abortion and just move on with the plan for our lives. No one would ever know. After the abortion I just felt relief. At the same time, I felt remorse knowing deep down I was not a real man because real men do not murder their children. I just tried to work and stay busy. So did she. Somehow, I knew if I slowed down enough to think about it, I would have to face what I had done to my fiancé and my baby. The funny thing is, I was not even sure WHY I was ashamed. This seemed to be the best decision for me and for her. This feeling of confusion lasted for the next 15 years!

Question #6: What about you changed the day of the abortion?

Answer: I knew deep in my heart I had wounded my future wife in such a way that only God could fix it and I remember crying at night and asking Him to help me make it right and heal our relationship. Trust had been broken on many levels and it took 15 years for it to be renewed. Now that we have God in our lives we have a whole new marriage but honestly, we still work on it to this day.

IT'S YOUR TURN TO TELL YOUR STORY!

_____

_____

_____

_____

_____

_____

_____

_____

_____

_____

_____

_____

_____

_____

_____

_____

_____

_____

_____

_____

_____

_____

_____

_____

_____
_____
_____
_____
_____
_____
_____
_____
_____
_____
_____
_____
_____
_____
_____
_____
_____
_____
_____
_____
_____

Contact us at www.surrenderingthesecret.com or stsfathersheart@gmail.com for questions or support.

STEP THREE: Understand The Truth About Abortion

Question #1: During the process of the abortion decision, was there ever a discussion about the development of the unborn child? The abortion procedure? Possible medical or emotional risk?

Answer: NO, we never discussed any of these issues we just set a date and went through the process of showing up having the abortion and going home and never speaking of it again.

Question #2: What thoughts or feelings did you have regarding the "procedure" itself?

Answer: When she walked out of the abortion room, I knew she would never be the same again. My heart was broken, and I tried to comfort her by doing anything she wanted. I was committed to never leaving her to deal with it by herself unless she wanted to be alone.

Question #3: Do you feel that you were "informed" about abortion in any way prior to the experience? What was your knowledge?

Answer: No, we were totally uninformed. We treated it like any other visit to the doctor. The Doctor always knows best, right? He is a professional and he has our best interest at heart. We later discovered that was not true at all. We walked in alone and we walked out alone.

Question #4: Do you feel that you have any symptoms of post abortion stress in your life now? Have you in the past?

Answer: No, through this healing process and doing the hard work it takes to confront a mistake like this one, we have received total healing in Jesus name! God saved our marriage. The first 9 years of our married life together were filled with resentment, fear, regret, depression, no self-discipline. I tried to cover-up what we had done by staying busy and never giving myself any time to think about it. Through this journey God has shown us how badly this decision has affected our entire lives but he has also shown us, He is a forgiving and healing God and wants His sons and daughters 'healed and whole in Him.

Your Response:

1. During the process of the abortion decision, was there ever a discussion about the development of the unborn child? The abortion procedure? Possible medical or emotional risk?

_____

_____

_____

_____

_____

_____

_____

_____

2. What thoughts or feelings did you have regarding the "procedure" itself?

_____

_____

_____

_____

_____

_____

_____

_____

3. Do you feel that you were "informed" about abortion in any way prior to the experience? What was your knowledge?

_____

_____

_____

_____

_____

_____

_____

_____

4. Do you feel that you have any symptoms of post abortion stress in your life now? Have you in the past?

_____

_____

_____

_____

_____

_____

_____

_____

STEP FOUR--- A Time for Anger

Question #1: Did you experience feelings of anger before the abortion experience?

Answer: Yes, I was angry with myself that I had broken trust and had no self-control. I had been so stupid as to not protect my fiancé.

Question #2: Have you since?

Answer: The healing process my wife and I experienced uncovered a lot of unresolved anger. We had experienced many things in our marriage that were directly related to this decision. It was not always a pretty, nor an easy process to walk through and face these kinds of reactions. Let's just say during this anger session one fluffy pillow was lost to the world as I used it to catch the brunt of my pent-up emotions. A process our leader used in this session really worked for me. It felt so good to get that out though and I was set free that day.

Question #3: As you listened to the women in the video how are you affected?

Answer: I have had many anger issues. Honestly, I am still angry today at the abortion industry, at the lies and the evil that it pours out in our communities and on our people. We call ourselves a cultured society, yet we kill the most innocent people in our world for a profit! As we study past cultures and we see how they sacrificed children and people in general we see that life hasn't changed all that much. We still murder the most innocent for a profit! This makes me very ANGRY! At the same time, God has shown me how to use that emotion for good by serving through a local crisis pregnancy center and helping other men get healed from a past abortion. I am now fighting the fight God's way.

Your Response:

1. Did you experience feelings of anger before the abortion experience?

_____

_____

_____

_____

_____

_____

_____

2. Have you since?

_____

_____

_____

_____

_____

_____

_____

3. If you have access to the Surrendering the Secret videos (lifeway.com) or even the story of a woman close to you who has experienced an abortion—how are you affected by hearing her story?

_____

_____

_____

_____

_____

_____

_____

_____

_____

_____

_____

_____

_____

_____

_____

_____

_____

_____

_____

MIKE AND PAT LAYTON

STEP FIVE--- It's TIME To Forgive!

Question #1: Do you feel that there is anyone you need to forgive about your abortion experience? Tell about it.

Answer: Not today I have by the Grace of God been able to forgive and move on with the call on my life to help end abortion.

Question #2: Does anyone need to forgive you?

Answer: The only person I have really felt concerned about receiving forgiveness from is my wife and she and I are healed. We have surrendered this secret and have moved from remorse to results! We serve together to do all we can to be sure no other young couple goes through this choice alone and without true and factual information.

Question #3: Does hearing a woman's story and emotions give you any new revelation about a woman's response to a man's part in the abortion choice?

Answer: I knew my part. I know the part of most men in this decision. Many of us are just as scared and just as confused as the woman. It broke my heart to hear the stories of the women in the video and to realize the heartbreak that is caused by abortion, for everyone!

Question #4: Do you feel that God has forgiven you of any part you had in an abortion choice?

Answer: Yes, I know I am forgiven and have taken on the responsibility to help other post abortive men to receive forgiveness and total healing by sharing my story.

Your Response:

1. Do you feel that there is anyone you need to forgive about your abortion experience? Tell about it.

_____

_____

_____

_____

_____

_____

_____

_____

_____

_____

_____

_____

_____

_____

_____

2. Does anyone need to forgive you?

    _____

    _____

    _____

    _____

    _____

    _____

3. Does hearing a woman's story and emotions give
    you any new revelation about a woman's response
    to a man's part in the abortion choice?

    _____

    _____

    _____

    _____

    _____

    _____

4. Do you feel that God has forgiven you of any part
    you had in an abortion choice?

    _____

    _____

    _____

    _____

    _____

"The greatest want of the world is the want of men - men who will not be bought or sold, men who in their inmost souls are true and honest, men who do not fear to call sin by its right name, men whose conscience is as true to duty as the needle to the pole, men who will stand for the right though the heavens fall."

EG White

STEP SIX—The Great Exchange

Question #1: Are you a Christian? How do you know? When did you experience a saving faith in Jesus Christ?

Answer: Yes, I am saved today with a true relationship with Jesus and the Father. But we were both "saved" at the time of our abortion but had little self-control. I'm a preacher's son and she was a good church girl who loved the Lord. Yet we still committed this sin. God's Word says ALL fall short of His Glory. We understand that the love of Jesus covers all of our sin. We are forgiven but now we are responsible to speak the truth in love in order to save others.

Question #2: Have you actually dealt with your abortion spiritually, one on one with Christ?

Answer: Yes, and I continue to be motivated by Him to help others deal with their abortion experience as a part of the call on my life. I love to serve others in this area as I feel a special understanding of how we make this life stealing choice and how much God wants to restore us.

Your Response:

1. Are you a Christian? How do you know? When did
   you experience a saving faith in Jesus Christ?

_____

_____

_____

_____

_____

_____

2. Have you actually dealt with your abortion
   spiritually, one on one with Christ?

_____

_____

_____

_____

_____

_____

_____

_____

_____

_____

_____

STEP SEVEN: A Time for Release

Question #1: Have you experienced the time of surrender or time of acknowledging the lost life of your unborn child?

Answer: Yes, it was very humbling and rewarding. To weep over my lost child and to be cleansed by tears of repentance, changed my life and gave me new purpose. I now see people who have walked this journey through the Holy Spirit and allow God's power to move mountains of shame and loss out of the lives of people who are hurting.

 Question #2: If you were to write a letter to your unborn child, what would you say to him or her to say goodbye?

Answer: I would say I am sorry for not being a man, a Father and a leader. I am sorry for being more concerned with being a man pleaser than a God pleaser. I am sorry for not protecting his mother and him. And I would ask for forgiveness and let him know that now because of him, his mother and I have dedicated the rest of our lives to saving babies and helping people heal from this mistake. I would tell him that his life has left a legacy that helps us make sure that no one God places IN OUR PATH has to be uneducated about abortion ever again!

NOTE: A time of "memorial" release, saying goodbye, making a final statement of love and repentance is a very healing moment.

If you are walking this journey with a friend or loved one—please watch the Surrendering the Secret Step 7 Video available at lifeway.com (the videos are available separately) for an idea of what this step might look like.

Contact us at www.surrenderingthesecret.com or stsfathershearts@gmail.com for questions or support.

Your Response:

1. Have you experienced the time of "release" "surrender" or "memorial" for your unborn child?

    _____

2. If you were to write a letter to your unborn child, what would you say to him or her to say goodbye?

    _____

    _____

    _____

    _____

    _____

    _____

    _____

    _____

    _____

    _____

    _____

STEP EIGHT: Share Hope and Truth!

Read Revelation 12:11 and consider your thoughts as you read below.

Question #1: Have you spoken out about abortion publicly? How? When? Where?

Answer: Yes, we have opened a Pregnancy Help Center in Illinois. We help people who are facing the choice for abortion every day. We share our story at churches and events and lead men and women through the healing process found in this book.

 Question #2: How do you participate in sharing the truth about abortion with those you love and influence today?

Answer: I love to talk to people about the truth about abortion and help them see that an unplanned pregnancy is not some kind of death sentence! It is not the unforgivable sin. God always sees, always knows and always is there to rescue us from our mistakes. I love people right where they are and help them through the process of receiving forgiveness and healing. As a couple or man to man, we tell them our story and show them what God has done for us and He wants to do the same for them.

Question #3: What role do you feel men have in the freedom of abortion?

Answer: We have sacrificed a generation of innocent children on the altar of selfishness and the mighty dollar. Greed and selfishness have turned men, even men in our churches away from God's plan for life. The blood of the unborn is on our hands and we will be held accountable! It is time for both men and women to seek healing and share the truth about abortion. It is time for us to take a stand not through political rhetoric but through the Word of God. We must speak through love and restoration, but we must speak.

Question #4: How do you feel men's rights as Fathers should be protected?

Answer: I believe every man should have the right to know if he is the Father of an unborn child. He should be given the opportunity to do the right thing, even if the woman does not want the child men should be given the opportunity to keep their children. They deserve the chance to support the woman throughout the pregnancy financially, spiritually and emotionally. I believe the Father, equally with the mother, should have the opportunity to choose life.

YOUR RESPONSE TO THIS PART OF YOUR HEALING
JOURNEY

1. Have you spoken out about abortion publicly? How?
   When? Where?

   _____

   _____

   _____

   _____

   _____

   _____

   _____

   _____

   _____

2. How do you participate in sharing the truth about
   abortion with those you love and influence today?

   _____

   _____

   _____

   _____

   _____

   _____

   _____

   _____

   _____

3. What role do you feel men have in the freedom of abortion?

_____

_____

_____

_____

_____

_____

_____

_____

4. How do you feel men's rights as Fathers should be protected?

_____

_____

_____

_____

_____

_____

_____

_____

_____

_____

A CLOSING CHALLENGE

The core of being a man is reflecting God, the Creator of the Universe. We are all created with a desire to know God. St. Augustine said, "You have made us for yourself, and our heart is restless until it rests in you." While both men and women are made in the image of God, men and women each have unique and distinct God-given roles, and each reflect to varying degrees different attributes of God.

Godly men are created to reflect Christ with an unselfish willingness to lay down our lives for others, the courage to stand against oppression and injustice and a willingness to be a protector of the weak. Men are to lead, guide, protect and model moral Godly behavior. When Men are obedient to fulfill their God-given role, all the Earth is blessed. Fellow countrymen can be at rest, knowing that men of God stand prepared to act on their behalf. Wives feel loved and secure and are encouraged to be the women of God He intended them to be. Daughters feel loved and protected and have no need to find security in arms other than their fathers, and boys are brought up seeing an example of Godliness in their fathers and - wanting to be like their fathers - grow up to be Godly men.

E.G. White wrote, "The greatest want of the world is the want of men - men who will not be bought or sold, men who in their inmost souls are true and honest, men who do not fear to call sin by its right name, men whose conscience

MIKE AND PAT LAYTON

is as true to duty as the needle to the pole, men who will stand for the right though the heavens fall."

God created men in His image. To create, to protect, to multiply. Godly men can have the greatest impact on their wives, sons and daughters. Men, single or married, can have an immeasurably positive impact on our society and culture.

The Bible talks about the men of Issachar who "understood the times and knew what Israel should do." We are called to be men who understand our times and know what we should do. As men, we must 'stand in the gap 'on behalf of the weakest, as Jesus did, because the devaluation of life always attacks the weakest among us: the unborn, the sick, the handicapped, the weak, the elderly, orphaned, the marginalized, the in-firmed.

Men must stand up for the weakest because we can. Ability to act implies a responsibility to act. As leaders, men of God, Priests and spiritual warriors, it is Men's role and calling to stand in the gap. We are not only to be warriors, but Holy warriors! The enemy knows this and will do all in his power to prevent us from becoming men of action. Tozer says, "...The devil's master strategy for us is not to kill us physically but to destroy our power to wage spiritual warfare." And one of his primary methods of distracting us from our role as Godly men is getting us to misuse our sexuality. The misuse of sex has ruined countless lives, toppled kingdoms and caused the death of hundreds of millions.

From Samson to David to today's headlines, male followers of God are seldom prepared to deal with sexual temptation. A man who is unprepared to deal with sexual temptation is a man who is in great danger of falling into sexual sin. A man who is carrying around with him the baggage of unconfessed, unforgiven, sexual immorality is a man who is not likely to be waging spiritual warfare.

One of the primary consequences of sexual immorality is unplanned pregnancies and subsequently, abortion. Pastor Scotty Vaughn says that "fathers are supposed to die for their children, not the other way around." And yet today, an estimated 56 million unborn babies die by abortion every year - killed because their fathers did not care or were not allowed to care.

Abortion undermines who we are as men. The act of abortion undermines the very soul of masculinity. It allows us to abandon the children we were created to protect to a horrible destruction and take sexual advantage of the women we were created to defend. How are we as men to respond? First, by embracing a holy lifestyle with regards to sex, and second, by discipling and encouraging others to be Godly men themselves.

Our culture has been very successful at discouraging men from participating in the abortion and sanctity of human life debate. "It's a woman's body, so it's a woman's issue. You have no say in the matter." NOTHING could be further from the truth. If men are to reclaim their role of being defenders and protectors and providers, it must start with the most important issue of our lifetime. The issue of life itself. When it comes to the sanctity of human life, men should be at the forefront, providing leadership to the Christian response to the Global Abortion Holocaust and the culture of death.

Ephesians 5:11says," *Take no part in unfruitful works of darkness, but instead expose them."* Unfruitful works of darkness". Just what does that mean? Unfruitfulness speaks of sterility, lacking life, or leading to death. Works of darkness means it does not come from the mind of God, but from the mind of the evil one. Satan is the father of lies and murder and death. As men, we are to have no part in evil, sinful behavior. Quite the opposite - we are to expose unfruitful works of darkness. In fact, we are commanded to do so.

We must realize that Satan uses our God-given sexual urges to set traps that often defeat us time after time. The sexual attack is one that comes against us 24 hours a day, seven days a week. I encourage you to take on this attack with a powerful Biblical counter-attack. The process of equipping, encouraging and educating men to take their role at the forefront of restoring the sanctity of human life and Biblical human sexuality needs to be an on-going, core aspect of the Church.

The Church needs men to become like David's Mighty Men - servant-warriors who are attracted to the person of Christ and committed to the cause of Christ. When men embrace their God-given roles, leading from their knees, confessing their sins one to another and bearing each other's burdens, they become a formidable force for good.

ABOUT THE AUTHORS

Mike and Pat Layton have been married for over forty years and have spent the past thirty plus sharing God's redemptive healing for the millions upon millions of men and women who have experienced the heartbreak of a past abortion. God protected them as a couple from the grim odds of surviving the choice for abortion while in college and led them through the same healing and restoration process that you will find in this book. Not long after that healing journey, together with a community of friends and their church family, they opened Tampa, Florida's first pregnancy resource center, which became one of the nation's busiest centers growing into a statewide abstinence education program, an adoption agency and a best-selling abortion recovery program called *Surrendering the Secret.*

Mike and Pat make their home near the North Georgia Mountains and their playground in the crystal clear waters of the Gulf Coast. They have three adult children, two lovely daughters-by-love and five grands.

A FEW ADDITIONAL RESOURCES

Abortion and the Heartache of Stolen Fatherhood (Heartbeat International)

Fatherhood Aborted by Guy Condon

promisekeeperscom
focusonthefamily.com
prolifeman.org

For Training as a Leader, Pastor or Counselor of Men's Healing through Healing a Fathers Heart Contact us at www.surrenderingthesecret.com or stsinternational15@gmail.com for questions or support.

OUR WRITING TEAM

Pat Layton, Co-Founder and President, Surrendering the Secret

Mike Layton, Co-Founder and COO, Surrendering the Secret

Ann Reed, Writer, American Family Association

Raul Reyes, Founder and President, Life Equip Global

Tim Schultz, Embracing Grace After abortion

Help *Heal* The Heartbreak of Abortion in Your Church and Community!

Sources believe as many as 40% of women of childbearing age have experienced a past abortion.

Women are hurting everywhere, often **silently.**

Will *you* lead the way?

Help give a *priceless* gift of healing to a woman
Share in her JOY when she experiences *freedom*
Create a lasting friendship
Share TRUTH

Say *YES* and make a difference!

If you are interested in providing STS through your church, counseling organization or pregnancy resource center please check out our website at www.surrenderingthesecret.com

IMPORTANT NOTE FOR THOSE SEEKING TO SHARE *A SURRENDERED LIFE*

The bottom line is that men need healing from abortion as much as women but they process their feelings and healing very differently.

For those women, family members or friends who have experienced an abortion and desire to share this journey with a man, here are a few ideas:

1) Be certain YOU are healed first. I had a mentor many years ago who shared these wise words with me "You can't give away what you do not have". Go through the healing process found in this book and the partnering Bible Study Surrendering the Secret with a friend, coach or Christian counselor. Seek your own healing before trying to help others.

2) Transparently share your own personal journey or experience. We always advise that the healing journey of abortion be shared with someone you trust, maybe by sharing your own process without having any expectations of the other person, God will begin His work in that persons heart.

3) Contact the Surrendering the Secret International headquarters by email or through our website for information regarding men's resources, healing retreats and couples healing.

4) Remember, you are not "The Healer", God is in charge and can handle the healing journey of your relative, spouse or friend. Join Him through prayer, patience and your own surrender.

A SURRENDERED
LIFE

Healing and Hope for Women,
Men and Couples After Abortion

PAT LAYTON

Made in the USA
Monee, IL
26 July 2020